HOW TO WORK FROM ANYWHERE

Your Guide to Thrive as a Remote Worker

By Estefania Hernandez

*How to Work From Anywhere:
Your Guide to Thrive as a Remote Worker*

Copyright © 2024 by Estefania Elena Hernandez Lopez All rights reserved.

No part of this book may be reproduced, distributed, or transmitted in any form or by any means, including photocopying, recording, or other electronic or mechanical methods, without the prior written permission of the publisher, except in the case of brief quotations embodied in critical reviews and certain other noncommercial uses permitted by copyright law.

Disclaimer: The information contained in this book is for general informational purposes only. The author and publisher make no representations or warranties of any kind, express or implied, about the completeness, accuracy, reliability, suitability, or availability with respect to the information, products, services, or related graphics contained in this book for any purpose. Any reliance you place on such information is therefore strictly at your own risk.

In no event will the author or publisher be liable for any loss or damage, including without limitation, indirect or consequential loss or damage, or any loss or damage whatsoever arising from loss of data or profits arising out of, or in connection with, the use of this book.

How to Work from Anywhere: The Ultimate Guide to Mastering Remote Work
ISBN: 9798333722027
First Edition: 2024

Contact Information:
For inquiries, interviews, or speaking engagements, please contact:
Estefania Hernandez
https://www.linkedin.com/in/estefaniahernandez/
estefdesigns.com

To all the remote workers and digital nomads who dare to explore the world while achieving their professional dreams.

Table Of Contents

Foreword — 7

PART I: Preparing for Remote Work — 12

Ch. 1: Understanding Remote Work — 13

Ch. 2: Are You Ready for Remote Work? — 19

Ch. 3: Setting Up Your Remote Office — 29

PART II: Finding Remote Work Opportunities — 51

Ch. 4: Job Search Strategies — 52

Ch. 5: Creating a Compelling Remote Work Application — 78

Chapter 6: Acing the Remote Job Interview — 88

PART III: Thriving as a Remote Worker — 100

Chapter 7: Time Management and Productivity — 101

Chapter 8: Communication and Collaboration Tools & Strategies — 117

Chapter 9: Maintaining Work-Life Balance — 127

PART IV: Advanced Remote Work Skills — 136

Chapter 10: Developing Technical Proficiency: — 137

Chapter 11: Building a Remote Work Community	151
Chapter 12: Remote Work Etiquette and Professionalism	162
PART V: Long-Term Success and Growth	174
Chapter 13:	175
Career Development in a Remote World	175
Chapter 14:	187
Managing Your Finances as a Remote Worker	187
Chapter 15:	202
Embracing a Remote Work Lifestyle	202
Conclusion	220

Foreword

The Rise of Remote Work: A Global Shift

Welcome to the exciting world of remote work! If you're reading this, you're likely curious about working from anywhere or already part of the growing remote workforce.

Let's start with some background on how remote work has taken the world by storm. Over the past few years, we've seen a massive shift in how people work. Thanks to technological advances and changes in how businesses operate, working remotely has become more popular than ever.

The COVID-19 pandemic accelerated this trend, pushing many companies to adopt remote work almost overnight.

What started as a temporary solution has become a lasting change for many of us. Working from home, a café, or even a beach on the other side of the world is more than a dream – it's a reality.

Benefits and Challenges of Remote Work

Remote work offers a lot of perks that can make your work life more enjoyable and balanced. For starters, you can say goodbye to long commutes and hello to a more flexible schedule. Imagine working in your pyjamas or setting up your office wherever you feel most productive – endless possibilities! Plus, remote work can help you better manage your work-life balance, giving you more time for family, hobbies, and self-care.

However, remote work isn't all sunshine and rainbows. It comes with its own set of challenges.

Without the traditional office environment, some people feel isolated and miss the daily interactions with coworkers. Communication can be trickier, and it's easy to blur the lines between work and personal time. Staying productive and motivated on your own can also be challenging. And let's remember the technical issues arising when you rely on your home internet and personal devices.

Purpose of the Book

That's where this book comes in. "*How to Work From Anywhere: Your Guide to Thrive as a Remote Worker*" is here to guide you through the ins and outs of remote work. Whether you're new to the concept, considering a switch, or already working remotely and looking to up your game, this book is packed with tips, tricks, and strategies to help you succeed.

What Readers Will Gain

So, what can you expect to gain from this book? Here's a sneak peek:

- **Understanding Remote Work:** We'll start by explaining remote work and helping you determine whether it fits you.
- **Setting Up Your Workspace:** Learn how to create a comfortable and productive home office that suits your needs.
- **Finding Remote Jobs:** Learn where to look for remote job opportunities and how to stand out in your applications.
- **Nailing the Interview:** Get insider tips on ace remote job interviews and showcase your skills.
- **Staying Productive:** Find out how to manage your time effectively, stay organized, and keep your productivity levels high.

- **Communication and Collaboration**: Master the art of virtual communication and working with remote teams.
- **Balancing Work and Life:** Learn strategies to maintain a healthy work-life balance and avoid Burnout.
- **Advanced Skills:** Dive into advanced topics like continuous learning, networking, and building a remote work community.
- **Long-Term Success:** Plan your remote career growth, manage your finances, and embrace the remote lifestyle.

By the end of this book, you'll have all the tools and knowledge you need to thrive as a remote worker. Whether working from your kitchen table or a tropical paradise, *"How to Work From Anywhere: Your Guide to Thrive as a Remote Worker"* will help you make the most of your remote work journey. Let's dive in!

PART I: Preparing for Remote Work

Chapter 1:
Understanding Remote Work

Definition and Types of Remote Work

Simply put, remote work is any work you can do outside a traditional office. Instead of commuting to a physical location daily, remote workers use technology to do their jobs from wherever they are. This could be at home, in a coffee shop, co-working space, or while travelling.

There are several types of remote work:

Fully Remote Jobs: These positions are entirely done from outside the office. Companies that hire for fully remote jobs might not have any physical offices.

Hybrid Remote Jobs: These roles combine remote work with some time spent in the office. Employees might work from home a few days a week and go to the office on other days.

Freelance/Contract Work: Freelancers and contractors are often remote workers who are hired for specific projects or periods. They might work for multiple clients and have a lot of flexibility in where and when they work.

Telecommuting: This is often used interchangeably with remote work, but it can also mean employees work from home temporarily or part-time.

Historical Context and Trends

Remote work isn't a new concept. It dates back to the days when artisans worked from home-based workshops.

However, the modern form of remote work began to gain traction in the 1970s and 1980s with the advent of personal computers and the Internet. The real boom came in the 2000s, as technology improved and more companies saw the potential benefits.

The rise of the digital age, with email, video conferencing, and cloud-based tools, made it easier for people to work from anywhere. Companies began recognizing that they could hire talent globally without geographic location constraints.

Then, in 2020, the COVID-19 pandemic hit, and remote work became necessary for millions. Companies that had never considered remote work had to adapt quickly.

This global shift proved that many jobs could be done just as effectively, if not more so, outside the traditional office. Remote work is here to stay, with many organizations adopting permanent remote or hybrid work models.

Myths and Misconceptions

Despite its growing popularity, remote work is still surrounded by myths and misconceptions. Let's debunk a few of the common ones:

Myth: Remote Workers Are Less Productive

Reality: Remote workers can be even more productive than those working in an office. Without the distractions of a bustling office and the time saved from commuting, many remote workers find they can focus better and get more done.

Myth: Remote Work Is Lonely

Reality: While remote workers miss out on the daily face-to-face interactions of an office, there are plenty of ways to stay connected. Regular video meetings, chat apps, and virtual team-building activities help maintain a sense of camaraderie and teamwork.

Myth: You Can't Advance Your Career Remotely

Reality: Career growth is absolutely possible in a remote setting. Many remote workers receive promotions, take on leadership roles, and find new opportunities. It's all about demonstrating your value, staying visible, and continuing to develop your skills.

Myth: Remote Workers Are Always Available

Reality: One of the biggest challenges of remote work is setting boundaries. Just because you're working from home doesn't mean you're on call 24/7. Establishing precise working hours and communicating them to your team is essential.

Remote work offers a world of possibilities, but it's essential to understand what it entails. By knowing the different types of remote work, appreciating its history, and separating fact from fiction, you'll be better prepared to thrive in this new way of working.

Chapter 2:

Are You Ready for Remote Work?

So, you're intrigued by the idea of remote work and all the freedom and flexibility it promises. But how do you know if it's the right fit for you? In this chapter, we'll explore the essential skills and traits you'll need, help you evaluate your readiness, and guide you in identifying your strengths and areas for improvement.

How to Self-Assess If You're Suitable for Remote Work

Remote work offers incredible flexibility and freedom but requires a specific skill set and mindset.

To determine if you're suitable for remote work, you can conduct a self-assessment focusing on critical areas such as motivation, time management, communication, tech proficiency, discipline, adaptability, problem-solving, and organization.

Here's a step-by-step guide to help you evaluate your readiness:

Step 1: Reflect on Essential Skills and Traits

Use the questions below to help you reflect on your strengths and weaknesses in various remote working skills.

Self-Motivation

- Do I have a solid drive to start and complete tasks without constant supervision?
- Am I good at setting personal goals and staying focused on achieving them?

Time Management

- Can I plan my day effectively and adhere to a schedule?
- Can I prioritize tasks and avoid distractions?

Communication Skills

- Am I comfortable using email, chat apps, and video calls for work communication?
- Do I proactively keep my team updated on my progress and any issues?

Tech Savvy

- Am I familiar with basic troubleshooting for my computer and the Internet?
- Can I quickly learn new software and tools?

Discipline

- Can I resist taking long breaks or handling personal tasks during work hours?
- Am I able to maintain focus even when working alone?

Adaptability

- Do I handle changes and new situations well?
- Am I open to learning and trying new ways of working?

Problem-Solving Skills

- Can I find solutions to problems without immediate help?
- Do I enjoy figuring things out on my own?

Organization

- Can I keep my work area and digital files neat and organized?
- Do I have a system for tracking tasks and deadlines?

Now, these questions aren't meant to discourage you. It's perfectly okay not to have a perfect score. What's more important is understanding your strengths and weaknesses so that you can develop strategies to ensure a successful remote working career.

Self-Assessment Quiz

Use the short quiz below to give you a quick overview of your general remote working skills. Rate yourself on a scale of 1 to 5 for each question (1 being "strongly disagree" and 5 being "strongly agree "):

1. I find it easy to start and finish tasks without needing external pressure.
2. I can plan my day and stick to my schedule effectively.
3. I am comfortable communicating with email, chat apps, and video calls.
4. I am familiar with basic troubleshooting for my computer and the Internet.
5. I can resist taking long breaks or handling personal tasks during work hours.
6. I handle changes and new situations well.
7. I can find solutions to problems without immediate help.
8. I keep my work area and digital files neat and organized.

Step 2: Analyze Your Results

Total Score:

- **35-40:** You are highly suited for remote work. You possess the necessary skills and traits to thrive in a remote environment.
- **25-34:** You have many qualities needed for remote work but may need to focus on improving specific areas.
- **15-24:** You might find remote work challenging and need to develop several skills to succeed.
- **Below 15:** Remote work might be easier with significant changes and improvements in critical areas.

Step 3: Identify Strengths and Areas for Improvement

Strengths

Identify the areas where you scored the highest. These are your strengths and can help you succeed in a remote work environment. For example, suppose you scored high in self-motivation and discipline. In that case, you're likely good at staying on track with your tasks without needing external pressure.

Areas for Improvement

Look at the areas where you scored the lowest. These are your growth opportunities. For instance, if you scored low in tech proficiency, you should invest time learning basic troubleshooting skills and familiarizing yourself with standard remote work tools.

Step 4: Create a Development Plan

Based on your self-assessment, create a plan to develop the skills and traits where you need improvement. Here are some ideas:

- **Time Management**: Use digital planners, to-do lists, and time-tracking apps to organize your workday.
- **Communication**: Practice using different communication tools and proactively update your team on progress.
- **Tech Proficiency**: Take online courses or watch tutorials to improve your tech skills.
- **Discipline**: Set specific work hours and create a dedicated workspace to minimize distractions.
- **Adaptability**: Try new work methods and be open to feedback to enhance flexibility.

By following these steps, you can clearly understand whether remote work is a good fit for you and identify what you need to do to prepare for a successful remote work experience. Remember, the goal is not to be perfect but to be aware of your strengths and continuously work on areas that need improvement.

By understanding your strengths and areas for improvement, you can take steps to develop the skills you need to thrive.

Chapter 3:
Setting Up Your Remote Office

Creating a comfortable and efficient home office is essential to thriving in a remote work environment. A well-thought-out workspace can boost productivity, enhance focus, and make your remote work experience more enjoyable.

Let's walk through the essentials of setting up your home office, including choosing the proper workspace, selecting essential tools and technology, and ensuring ergonomics and comfort.

Choosing the Righ Workspace

Find a Dedicated Area

A dedicated workspace helps you separate work from personal life, making it easier to focus and maintain boundaries. Having a specific space for work boosts your focus and productivity, making it easier to get into a professional mindset. It also helps you stay organized and reduces distractions, improving efficiency.

Plus, a well-defined work area can help you maintain a better work-life balance and avoid the blurring of boundaries that often happens when working from home.

Tips for Choosing:

- **Quiet Zone**: Pick a spot away from household distractions and noise. A spare room or a quiet corner works well.
- **Good Lighting**: Choose a location with plenty of natural light or invest in good-quality desk lamps to keep your workspace bright and inviting.
- **Accessibility**: Ensure your chosen spot is easily accessible and has adequate work materials and equipment space.

Personalize Your Space

A personalized workspace can make you feel more comfortable and motivated. Personalizing your work area is important because it makes your space more enjoyable and comfortable, boosting your mood and productivity.

Adding personal touches like photos, artwork, or plants can make your workspace feel inviting and uniquely yours. Staying motivated and focused is more accessible when surrounded by things that make you happy. Plus, a personalized space can help you feel more connected to your work, even if you're miles away from a traditional office.

Tips for Personalizing:

- **Decorate**: Add personal touches like artwork, plants, or photos to make the space feel more like yours.
- **Storage**: Use shelves, drawers, or organizers to keep your workspace tidy and efficient. Having everything you need within arm's reach can enhance your productivity.

Renting a Co-Working Space

If your office or clients are in a different city (or even country) than yours, consider renting a desk at a co-working space. A co-working space is a shared office environment where individuals from other companies, freelancers, and remote workers come together.

These spaces provide a professional setting with amenities like desks, meeting rooms, high-speed Internet, and office equipment.

Co-working spaces can foster community and collaboration, often offering networking events, workshops, and social activities. They are designed to provide a flexible and productive workspace for people who might otherwise work from home or coffee shops.

Finding the perfect co-working space can significantly affect how enjoyable and productive your remote work experience is. Given the many options available, choosing a space that fits your needs and preferences is key.

Here are some tips to help you pick the right space for you:

1. Know What You Need

Think About Your Work Style

Your work style will help determine what space best supports your productivity. Different co-working spaces offer different settings and vibes, such as noise levels, amenities (like meeting rooms), and social opportunities.

Questions to Ask Yourself:

- Do you need a quiet place to focus, or do you prefer a lively, collaborative environment?
- Will you need private meeting rooms or just a desk where you can plug in and work?

Set Your Budget

Knowing your budget helps narrow your choices and avoid overspending. Co-working spaces come in all shapes and sizes, from super-fancy executive buildings to cozy local neighbourhood workspaces. There's a co-working space out there for every budget.

Questions to Ask Yourself:

- How much are you willing to spend each month?
- Are you okay with paying extra for amenities or services?

Extra tip: When checking co-working prices, remember to consider taxes. Often, the advertised price doesn't include them.

2. Consider the Location

Proximity to Home

A space close to home makes commuting more accessible and convenient. After all, one of the advantages of remote work is that it avoids unnecessary and dreadfully long commutes.

Questions to Ask Yourself:

- How far is the co-working space from your home?
- Is it easily accessible by public transport or do you need parking?

Neighbourhood Perks

The neighbourhood can enhance your experience with amenities like coffee shops, libraries, or supply stores. It also adds to the lifestyle aspect of working remotely.

Questions to Ask Yourself:

- Are there good places to eat, shop, or relax nearby?
- Is the area safe and comfortable to be in?

3. Check Out the Facilities and Amenities

Basic Needs

Essential facilities are necessary for your day-to-day work. When deciding on a co-working space, ask the staff to tour you, and don't be afraid to ask questions. You want to ensure that the facilities are well-kept and clean and that the equipment (such as meeting room screens, printers, copy machines, and air conditioning) works.

Questions to Ask:

- Does the space have high-speed Internet, comfortable chairs, and a clean environment?
- Are there basic amenities like a kitchen, coffee machine, and restrooms?

Extras

Additional perks can make your experience more enjoyable and valuable. For example, you might want to freeze your membership if you go away for a month to travel. However, this might affect the pricing of the co-working space. You will need to decide which extra amenities are must-haves and which ones you can live without.

Questions to Ask:

- Are there meeting rooms, phone booths, or event spaces available?
- Does the space offer extras like networking events, workshops, or wellness programs?

4. Feel the Atmosphere

Work Environment

The atmosphere affects your productivity and satisfaction. Remember to consider your gut feeling. When assessing a new co-working space, look around and see other people working there. Do they look happy? Does it feel like a welcoming atmosphere? You will likely spend a lot of time working from this space, so it's essential that you feel comfortable and welcomed.

Questions to Ask:

- Is the space designed for quiet work or collaboration?
- Is it clean, well-organized, and comfortable?

Community Vibe

A friendly community can make your workday more enjoyable. A co-working space can be a wonderful place to meet new people and network.

Questions to Ask:

- Does the space have events or social activities that help you connect with other members?
- Are the staff and other members welcoming and supportive?

5. Review Membership Options

Reviewing membership options for co-working spaces is essential because it helps you find the best fit for your needs and budget.

Co-working spaces offer various plans, from daily drop-ins to monthly memberships, each with different perks and costs.

By comparing these options, you can choose a plan that suits your work style, whether you need occasional access or a full-time desk. This way, you ensure you get the most value from your membership and find a co-working space that aligns with your work habits and goals.

Questions to Ask:

- What types of memberships are available (e.g., hot desk, dedicated desk, private office)?
- What are the terms for flexibility, like changing plans or cancelling?

6. Read Reviews and Ask for Recommendations

Checking online reviews and recommendations for co-working spaces is essential because it helps you understand what to expect before you commit. Reviews from other remote workers can give you insights into the space's atmosphere, amenities, and overall vibe.

They can also highlight potential issues or perks that might initially be obscure. By reading these reviews, you can make a more informed decision and choose a co-working space that best fits your needs and preferences.

Questions to Ask:

- What do online reviews say about the space's amenities and overall environment?
- Are there common positives or issues mentioned?
- Do friends or colleagues have recommendations for co-working spaces?
- Are there local groups or online communities where you can get advice?

7. Try It Out

Some co-working spaces offer daily drop-ins so you can test the waters. Others let you sign up month-to-month or for a few months before committing to a longer term. Try the space first to ensure it's the right fit before committing to a long-term contract.

By following these simple steps, you'll be able to find a co-working space that suits your needs, fits your budget, and enhances your work experience.

Essential Tools and Technology

Reliable Internet Connection

A solid and stable internet connection is crucial for video calls, accessing cloud-based documents, and staying connected with your team.

Tips:

- **Upgrade Your Plan**: Consider upgrading to a higher-speed plan if you frequently experience slow speeds or connectivity issues.
- **Wi-Fi Router**: Position your router in a central location and invest in a good-quality router to improve signal strength.

Computer and Accessories

Your computer is the heart of your remote work setup. High-quality accessories can enhance your comfort and efficiency.

Tips:

- **Computer:** Ensure your computer is up-to-date and capable of handling your work tasks smoothly.
- **Keyboard and Mouse:** Use a comfortable keyboard and mouse to reduce strain. Ergonomic models can help prevent repetitive stress injuries.
- **Look into financial advantages:** This will vary depending on where you live and your company. Some governments offer tax benefits to freelancers and business owners for buying office equipment. Many companies also provide a budget for setting up your home office.

Software and Tools

The right software and tools can make remote work more efficient and seamless. It's also worth noting that there are free options to help you get started, like Canva for design purposes and Google Suite, which includes Google Docs and Google Sheets - Google's free version of Microsoft Word and Excel.

Tips:

- **Communication Tools**: Use Slack, Microsoft Teams, or Zoom for effective communication and collaboration.
- **Productivity Tools**: Tools like Trello, Asana, or Google Workspace can help you organize tasks and manage projects efficiently.

Ergonomics and Comfort

Ergonomic Furniture

Proper ergonomics help prevent discomfort and health issues from prolonged sitting. By properly arranging your workstation, you can reduce physical strain and improve productivity.

Tips:

- **Chair and Desk Height:** Make sure your chair and desk are at the right height. Your feet should be flat on the floor, and your knees should be at a 90-degree angle. Your desk should allow your arms to be at a comfortable angle with your elbows at 90 degrees when typing.

- **Monitor Position:** Place your monitor at eye level, about an arm's length away. This helps prevent neck strain. The top of the screen should be at or just below eye level, so you don't have to tilt your head up or down.
- **Keyboard and Mouse Placement:** Keep your keyboard and mouse close to each other and at the same level. Your wrists should be straight, and your hands should be at or below elbow level. Use a wrist rest if needed to maintain a neutral wrist position.

Breaks and Movement

Regular breaks and movement can prevent stiffness and promote well-being.

Tips:

- **Stand Up:** Set a timer to remind yourself to stand up, stretch, or walk around every hour.
- **Stretching:** Incorporate simple stretches and exercises to relax your muscles and reduce tension.

Setting up your remote office isn't just about finding a workplace; it's about creating a space that boosts your productivity, comfort, and overall well-being. By carefully choosing your workspace, equipping it with essential tools and technology, and focusing on ergonomics, you'll be well on your way to a successful remote work experience.

PART II: Finding Remote Work Opportunities

Chapter 4:
Job Search Strategies

Finding the right remote job can be an exciting journey. Still, knowing where and how to look is essential to ensure you're targeting the best opportunities. This chapter will cover identifying legitimate remote job listings, networking effectively, and using specialized job boards to your advantage. Let's explore the strategies to help you land your ideal remote position.

1. Identifying Legitimate Remote Job Listings

Spotting Red Flags

Ensuring job listings are legit is crucial for remote workers to avoid scams and wasted time.

Verifying the authenticity of job postings helps you steer clear of fraudulent offers and empowers you, ensuring you're applying to reputable companies and taking control of your job search.

It's essential to check for red flags like vague job descriptions that lack specific responsibilities or requirements, requests for personal information upfront, or jobs that seem too good to be true, such as high salaries for minimal work.

By taking these precautions, you can protect yourself and focus on finding genuine opportunities that match your skills and career goals.

What to Look For:

- **Company Reputation:** Check if the company has a solid online presence and positive reviews. Look for company websites and profiles on LinkedIn.
- **Job Details:** Genuine job listings will clearly describe job responsibilities, required skills, and salary ranges. Be wary of vague listings or promise high salaries for minimal work.

How to Verify a Job Listing:

- **Direct Company Websites:** Apply through the company's official website rather than third-party sites whenever possible.

- **Research**: Use sites like Glassdoor or Indeed to read reviews and verify the legitimacy of the company and its job postings.

What to Avoid:

- **Upfront Fees**: Avoid jobs that require you to pay for training, equipment, or application fees.
- **Unrealistic Promises**: Jobs that promise unrealistic income or require minimal effort are often red flags.

2. Networking and Leveraging Social Media

Build a Strong LinkedIn Profile

LinkedIn is a powerful tool for showing off your skills and connecting with potential employers. It allows you to network with professionals from various industries, expand your professional circle and increase your chances of finding remote job opportunities through referrals and recommendations.

You can think of your LinkedIn profile as an online resume or portfolio showcasing your skills, experience, and achievements. A well-crafted profile can attract recruiters and hiring managers looking for remote talent.

A strong LinkedIn profile is essential for attracting potential employers and building a professional network. Here are some steps to help you create an impressive LinkedIn profile:

Profile Picture

- **Choose a Professional Photo**: Use a high-quality, professional-looking headshot where you are dressed appropriately for your industry.
- **Smile and Be Approachable**: A friendly, approachable expression can make a positive impression.

Headline

- **Be Clear and Specific:** Your headline should clearly state your professional role and key skills. For example, "Remote Marketing Specialist | Content Creator | Social Media Expert."

Summary

- **Write a Compelling Summary**: Your summary should briefly describe who you are, what you do, and what makes you unique. Highlight your key achievements and skills. Use a friendly yet professional tone.
- **Include Keywords**: Incorporate keywords related to your industry and desired job roles to make your profile more searchable.

Experience

- **Detail Your Job Roles**: List your current and past job roles, briefly describing your responsibilities and achievements.
- **Use Bullet Points**: Bullet points make your information easy to read and scan.

- **Include Results:** Where possible, quantify your achievements (e.g., "Increased social media engagement by 30%").

Skills and Endorsements

- **List Relevant Skills**: Add skills that are relevant to your profession. LinkedIn allows you to list up to 50 skills.
- **Get Endorsements**: Ask colleagues and connections to endorse your skills. Endorsements can enhance your profile's credibility.

Recommendations

- **Request Recommendations:** Ask former colleagues, supervisors, or clients to write recommendations for you. Positive testimonials can significantly enhance your profile.

- **Give Recommendations**: Write recommendations for others. Often, they will reciprocate.

Education

- **List Your Education**: Include your educational background, degrees, and relevant certifications or courses.
- **Add Descriptions**: If applicable, provide a brief description of your coursework, projects, or achievements.

Licenses and Certifications

- **Add Certifications:** Include any relevant certifications and licenses. This can include professional development courses and online certifications from platforms like LinkedIn Learning or Coursera.

Volunteer Experience

- **Include Volunteer Experience:** If you have any volunteer experience, add it to your profile. It shows a well-rounded character and additional skills.

Accomplishments

- **Highlight Projects and Publications:** If you have completed significant projects, written articles, or received awards, include them in the Accomplishments section.

Engage and Connect

- **Join Groups:** Participate in LinkedIn groups related to your industry to network and stay updated on trends.

- **Post and Share Content**: Regularly share articles, updates, and content to keep your profile active and engaging.
- **Connect with Purpose**: Send personalized connection requests to people you meet professionally, ensuring you build a meaningful network.

Profile URL

- **Customize Your URL:** You can customize your LinkedIn profile URL to make it cleaner and more professional (e.g., linkedin.com/in/yourname).

Keep It Updated

- **Regular Updates:** To keep your profile current and relevant, regularly update it with new skills, experiences, and accomplishments.

By following these steps, you can build a strong LinkedIn profile highlighting your professional background, skills, and achievements. This will help you stand out as an attractive candidate for remote work opportunities.

Join Professional Groups and Forums

Joining professional groups and forums is important for remote workers because they offer valuable networking opportunities and support. These communities can help you stay updated on industry trends, share tips and resources, and, most importantly, connect with other remote professionals, fostering a sense of community and belonging.

Engaging in these groups can provide advice, solve problems, and even lead to new job opportunities. Plus, being part of a professional network helps you feel less isolated and more connected to your field.

How to Join:

- **LinkedIn Groups**: Participate in groups related to your field to stay updated on industry trends and job openings.
- **Online Forums**: Engage in forums like Reddit or specialized industry forums where remote jobs are frequently discussed.

Use Social Media Wisely

Social media is an excellent tool for remote workers because it helps them connect with industry peers and potential employers from anywhere. Platforms like LinkedIn and X let you join relevant groups, follow influential figures, and share your expertise.

This strategic use of social media helps you stay informed about job opportunities and industry trends. It keeps you engaged, opening doors to new collaborations, advice, and career growth.

Tips for Social Media:

- **Follow Companies:** Follow companies you're interested in on platforms like X or Facebook to stay updated on job postings.

- **Join Relevant Groups**: Look for Facebook groups or X chats related to remote work and industry-specific topics.

Remote Job Boards and Websites

Explore Remote Job Boards

Remote job boards are specialized websites listing job opportunities for remote work. These platforms help job seekers find positions that allow them to work from anywhere, whether from home, a co-working space, or while travelling.

They typically feature various roles across different industries and experience levels, making finding remote jobs matching your skills and preferences easier.

Some popular remote job boards include FlexJobs, Remote.co, and We Work Remotely.

Top Remote Job Boards:

- **We Work Remotely**: Offers various remote job listings across multiple fields.
- **Remote.co**: Provides remote job listings and valuable resources for remote workers.
- **FlexJobs**: Features vetted remote and flexible job listings focusing on quality and legitimacy.

Use Niche Job Websites

Niche websites can help you find specialized roles that match your skills and interests.

Examples:

- **AngelList:** Great for finding remote positions at startups and tech companies.
- **Hubstaff Talent:** A free resource for finding remote jobs, freelance gigs, and contract work.

Regularly Check Job Listings

Checking increases your chances of finding new opportunities.

Tips for Regular Checking:

- **Set Up Alerts**: Use job board features to set up email alerts for new remote job postings.
- **Be Persistent**: Make it a habit to check job boards and company websites regularly.

How to Negotiate Remote Working Conditions at Your Current Job

Suppose you already have a remote-friendly job, like a UX Designer, Writer, or Software Engineer. In that case, it's worth talking to your boss about possibly working remotely.

Negotiating remote working conditions can be a great way to enhance your work-life balance and boost your productivity. If you're considering switching to remote work or adjusting your current remote setup, thoughtfully approaching the conversation with your employer can make all the difference.

How to negotiate your remote working conditions:

1. Prepare Your Case

Understand Your Reasons

Clearly defining why you want to work remotely will help you communicate your needs effectively.

Questions to Consider:

- How will remote work benefit your productivity and job performance?
- Are there specific personal or professional reasons that make remote work appealing?

2. Gather Supporting Evidence

Providing evidence or examples can strengthen your case and show that remote work is feasible.

What to Include:

- **Successful Remote Examples:** Share examples of how remote work has been successful for others in similar roles or within your company.
- **Productivity Data:** If possible, present data showing your productivity and performance when working remotely or highlight your achievements.

3. Choose the Right Time

Picking the right moment can increase the likelihood of a positive outcome.

Best Times to Approach:

- **Performance Reviews**: During a performance review or one-on-one meeting, your manager is already focused on your performance and career development.
- **After a Successful Project**: When you've just completed a successful project or milestone, it's easier to make a case for why remote work will continue to benefit you and the company.

4. Propose a Plan

Be Specific

A clear plan shows you've thought about how remote work will be implemented and managed.

What to Include:

- **Schedule**: Suggest a specific remote work schedule (e.g., a full-time remote, hybrid model with certain days in the office).
- **Communication**: Outline how you will stay in touch with your team, such as through regular check-ins, video calls, and updates.

5. Address Potential Concerns

Anticipating and addressing potential concerns shows you're proactive and considerate of the company's needs.

Common Concerns:

- **Availability:** Reassure your manager about your availability and responsiveness during working hours.

- **Collaboration**: Explain how you will ensure effective cooperation and maintain team dynamics despite being remote.

6. Communicate Effectively

Use Clear and Positive Language

Clear, positive communication helps make your request seem reasonable and well-considered.

How to Communicate:

- **Focus on Benefits**: Emphasize how remote work will benefit both you and the company, such as increased productivity or better work-life balance.
- **Be Open and Flexible**: Show that you're open to negotiating the terms and willing to find a solution that works for everyone.

7. Prepare for Questions and Feedback

Being prepared for questions and feedback helps you respond confidently and address any concerns.

Potential Questions:

- How will you handle tasks that require in-person presence?
- What measures will you take to ensure productivity and team engagement?

8. Follow Up

Formalize the Agreement

Putting the agreement in writing helps avoid misunderstandings and ensures both parties are on the same page.

What to Do:

- **Document the Details**: Once you've reached an agreement, summarize the terms in an email or formal document and ask your manager for confirmation.
- **Review and Adjust**: Agree on a review period to assess how the remote work arrangement is going and make adjustments if needed.

9. Show Appreciation

Expressing gratitude helps maintain a positive relationship with your employer.

What to Do:

- **Thank Your Manager:** Show appreciation for their willingness to consider your request and work with you on a solution.

- **Demonstrate Commitment**: Continue to perform at a high level and demonstrate that remote work benefits you and the company.

Negotiating remote working conditions can be smooth with preparation and clear communication.

By presenting a well-thought-out plan and addressing potential concerns, you can increase your chances of a successful outcome and enjoy the benefits of a remote work arrangement.

Using these strategies, you can effectively navigate the remote job market, identify genuine opportunities, and connect with potential employers. Remember to stay proactive, leverage your network, and use specialized job boards to find the perfect remote job.

Chapter 5:
Creating a Compelling Remote Work Application

Landing a remote job requires more than just a great resume. You need to create a compelling application that highlights your skills and shows why you're the perfect fit for a remote work environment. In this chapter, we'll walk through how to tailor your resume, write effective cover letters, and build a solid online presence to boost your chances of landing your dream remote job.

Tailoring Your Resume for Remote Positions

Highlight Remote-Related Skills

Remote work requires specific skills like project and task management and tech proficiency.

What to Include:

- **Technical Skills**: List relevant technical skills, like proficiency with remote collaboration tools (e.g., Slack, Zoom, Trello) and software specific to your field.
- **Soft Skills**: Emphasize skills like communication, time management, and problem-solving, which are essential for remote work.

Showcase Relevant Experience

Demonstrating past experience with remote or flexible work shows you're accustomed to managing tasks independently.

How to Present It:

- **Remote Work Experience**: If you've worked remotely before, highlight it prominently. Describe the tasks you handled and how you managed them effectively.
- **Freelance or Contract Work**: Include any freelance or contract work that requires self-discipline and remote collaboration.

Customize for Each Job

Tailoring your resume to each job application increases relevance and makes you stand out.

How to Customize:

- **Keywords:** Use keywords from the job description to match your resume with what the employer wants.
- **Achievements:** Highlight achievements and responsibilities that match the specific requirements of the remote job you're applying for.

Writing Effective Cover Letters

Start with a Strong Introduction

The introduction sets the vibe for your cover letter and grabs the employer's attention.

How to Write It:

- **Personalize It**: If possible, address the letter to the hiring manager by name. Mention the specific position you're applying for and why you're excited about it.
- **Highlight Key Skills**: Briefly introduce the key skills and experiences that make you a strong candidate for the remote position.

Demonstrate Remote Work Readiness

Showing you're prepared for the remote work environment helps convince the employer of your suitability.

How to Show Readiness:

- **Discuss Remote Work Experience:** Share examples of how you've successfully worked remotely or managed tasks independently.
- **Explain Your Remote Work Setup:** Mention how you've set up your home office or your strategies for staying productive and connected.

Conclude with a Call to Action

Ending with a clear call to action encourages the employer to take the next step in the hiring process.

How to Conclude:

- **Express Enthusiasm:** Reiterate your interest in the role and how excited you are about the opportunity.

- **Request an Interview**: Kindly ask for an interview to talk about how your skills match the job requirements.

Building a Strong Online Presence

Polish Your LinkedIn Profile

We already touched upon this point extensively in Chapter 4. However, just to review:

How to Polish Your LinkedIn Profile:

- **Complete Your Profile:** Ensure your LinkedIn profile is up-to-date with a professional photo, a detailed summary, and a comprehensive list of skills and experiences.

- **Showcase Remote Skills**: Highlight remote work experience, relevant skills, and any endorsements or recommendations that reinforce your suitability for remote roles.

Engage with Online Communities

Being active in professional communities can increase visibility and open networking opportunities.

How to Engage:

- **Join Relevant Groups**: Participate in LinkedIn groups or forums related to your industry or remote work.
- **Share Insights**: Post articles, comment on industry trends, and share your expertise to build your reputation as a knowledgeable professional.

Create a Personal Website or Portfolio

A personal website or portfolio is a great way to showcase your work, skills, and achievements. It's especially important for careers that need a visual review of your past work and process, like UX Design.

How to Create It:

- **Include Key Information:** Feature your resume, work samples, and any testimonials or case studies highlighting your achievements.
- **Keep It Professional:** Ensure your website is well-designed, easy to navigate, and reflects your personal brand and professional skills.

- **Use Platforms that offer pre-built websites:** Try using platforms that provide pre-built websites, like Wix and Squarespace. They're perfect if you want to create a site without coding skills. Alternatively, you can showcase your work professionally on sites like Behance and Dribble, which let you display your portfolio without designing and building a site from scratch.

By tailoring your resume, writing compelling cover letters, and building a solid online presence, you can create a remote work application that stands out from the crowd. These elements work together to showcase your suitability for remote roles and demonstrate your commitment to thriving in a remote work environment.

Chapter 6:

Acing the Remote Job Interview

Landing a remote job interview is exciting, but preparing is essential to making a solid impression. Whether conducted via video or phone, remote interviews have their own considerations. In this chapter, we'll cover common interview questions for remote positions, how to demonstrate your remote work competencies and tips for smoothly handling video and phone interviews.

Common Interview Questions for Remote Positions

Anticipating and preparing for common questions can help you respond confidently and effectively.

Common Questions:

- **"How do you stay motivated while working remotely?":** Discuss your strategies for self-discipline and maintaining productivity.
- **"Can you describe a time when you faced a challenge working remotely and how you overcame it?":** Provide examples of challenges you've faced and solutions you've implemented.
- **"How do you handle communication and collaboration with a remote team?":** Explain your approach to staying connected and working effectively with colleagues from a distance.

Answer with Relevant Examples

Using specific examples helps to illustrate your skills and experiences.

How to Answer:

- **Be Specific:** Describe concrete situations where you demonstrated relevant skills.
- **Use the STAR Method:** Structure your answers with Situation, Task, Action, and Result to provide clear and detailed responses.

Demonstrating Remote Work Competencies

Showcase Key Skills

Highlighting skills specific to remote work shows you're well-suited for a virtual environment.

Key Competencies:

- **Self-motivation:** Describe how you set and achieve goals independently.
- **Time Management:** Explain your methods for managing your schedule and meeting deadlines without direct supervision.
- **Tech Savvy:** Discuss your familiarity with remote tools and platforms, like video conferencing software, project management tools, and communication apps.

Emphasize Communication Skills

Good communication is key in remote work settings.

How to Emphasize:

- **Clarity and Regular Updates:** Talk about informing your team and ensuring clear communication.
- **Active Listening:** Share examples of listening carefully and responding thoughtfully in a remote context.

Demonstrate Problem-Solving Abilities

Remote work often requires solving issues independently.

How to Demonstrate:

- **Examples of Problem-Solving:** Provide instances where you successfully addressed challenges independently or with minimal supervision.
- **Adaptability:** Illustrate how you adapt to new tools or changes in workflow.

Keep critical information at hand.

Keep your resume, cover letter, and portfolio with relevant projects nearby. They come in handy if you need to share your screen to walk the client through a specific use case or if the interviewer asks for any of these documents.

Tips for Video Interviews

Set Up Your Space

A clean, quiet, professional environment helps you make a good impression. A calm, interruption-free environment lets you stay focused and present during the interview.

Also, proper lighting and sound setup make it easier for the interviewer to see and hear you clearly, facilitating better communication.

What to Do:

- **Choose a Quiet Location:** Ensure there's minimal background noise and distractions.
- **Use a Professional Background:** A tidy and neutral background looks more polished and keeps the focus on you.

Check Your Tech

Technical issues can disrupt the flow of the interview. Testing your equipment and internet connection beforehand ensures that technical issues don't disturb the interview.

What to Do:

- **Test Your Equipment:** Check your camera, microphone, and internet connection beforehand.
- **Familiarize yourself with the Platform:** Ensure you're comfortable using the video conferencing software.

Practice Good Etiquette

Professional behaviour helps create a positive impression.

What to Do:

- **Dress Professionally:** Dress just like you would for an in-person interview to show your commitment and Professionalism.
- **Be on time:** Few things look worse than being late for a job interview. Sign in to the virtual meeting a few minutes early.
- **Be prepared:** Considering the previous points, it's essential to go into the interview fully prepared. This helps you make a good impression on your potential employer or client, boost your confidence, and prevent mishaps.

Phone Interview Tips

Find a Quiet Place

Clear communication is vital in phone interviews.

What to Do:

- **Choose a Quiet Room**: Make sure there are no interruptions or background noise.
- **Use a Good Quality Phone**: Ensure your phone is in good working condition and fully charged.

Prepare Your Talking Points

Having your key points handy helps you stay focused and articulate.

What to Do:

- **Keep a Resume and Notes Nearby**: Have your resume and any notes or questions in front of you for quick reference.
- **Practice Speaking Clearly**: Speak clearly and at a comfortable pace to ensure you're easy to understand.

Follow Up Professionally - Send a Thank-You Note

A follow-up email demonstrates your enthusiasm and Professionalism.

After the interview, send a brief email thanking the interviewer for their time and reiterating your interest in the role.

By preparing for common remote work interview questions, highlighting your remote work skills, and using these tips for video and phone interviews, you'll make a great impression and boost your chances of landing that remote job you're aiming for.

PART III: Thriving as a Remote Worker

Chapter 7:

Time Management and Productivity

In the realm of remote work, you wield the power to shape your own time, a freedom that comes with the responsibility of maintaining productivity sans the confines of a traditional office. In this chapter, we'll review practical tips and tricks, empowering you to master time management and amplify productivity, maximizing your remote work experience.

Mastering Time Management as a Remote Worker

Working remotely allows you to create your own schedule. Still, it also requires a high level of discipline to manage your time effectively.

Without the traditional office structure, it's easy to procrastinate or get overwhelmed by tasks.

Here's are some tips to help you master time management and boost your productivity as a remote worker:

1. Set Clear Goals

Setting clear goals is a game-changer for staying focused and motivated as a remote worker. These goals not only help you prioritize tasks and keep distractions at bay but also provide a clear sense of direction and purpose. They serve as a compass, guiding your progress and keeping you engaged with your work.

The sight of your efforts contributing to these goals can be a powerful motivator, keeping you energized and on track throughout your day.

How to do it:

- **Daily Goals:** Start each day by outlining what you need to accomplish. Prioritize your tasks so you know which ones are the most important.
- **Weekly Goals:** Plan out your week in advance. This helps you allocate time for larger projects and ensures you work towards your long-term objectives.
- **Long-Term Goals:** Keep your big-picture goals in mind. Break them into smaller, manageable tasks you can work on regularly.

2. Create a Schedule

Creating a schedule is a lifesaver for time management when working remotely. It helps you structure your day to stay on top of tasks and avoid those "where did the time go?" moments.

A solid schedule keeps you organized, ensures you meet deadlines, and helps balance work with breaks. Additionally, having a plan in place means you can set aside dedicated time for both work and personal activities, making your day run smoothly and reducing stress.

Here are some tips:

- **Consistent Work Hours:** Try to start and end work at the same time every day. This creates a routine and helps you stay disciplined.
- **Time Blocking:** Divide your day into blocks of time dedicated to specific tasks. For example, reserve mornings for deep work and afternoons for meetings and administrative tasks.

- **Breaks:** Schedule regular breaks to rest and recharge. A popular approach is the Pomodoro Technique, which involves working for 25 minutes and then taking a 5-minute break.

3. Use a Planner or Digital Tools

Using a planner and digital tools to manage your time as a remote worker is a smart move. A planner helps you jot down your daily tasks and keep track of your goals in one place.

At the same time, digital tools offer handy features like reminders, deadlines, and calendar syncing. Together, they help you stay organized and on top of your work, making prioritizing tasks and managing your schedule easy.

Here is how to do it:

- **Daily Planner:** A physical planner can help you organize your tasks and visualize your schedule.
- **Digital Tools:** Apps like Trello, Asana, or Todoist can help you manage your tasks and collaborate with your team. You can also use calendar apps like Google Calendar to schedule meetings and reminders.

4. Prioritize Tasks

Not all tasks are created equal, so it's critical to prioritize them for better time management as a remote worker. By identifying which tasks are most urgent or essential, you can tackle the high-impact items first and avoid getting bogged down by less critical tasks.

Prioritizing helps you focus your energy where needed most, keeps you on track with deadlines, and ensures you're making meaningful progress on your big goals. This way, you'll feel more accomplished and in control of your workload.

Tools to help you prioritize your tasks:

- **Eisenhower Matrix:** This tool helps you categorize tasks into four quadrants: urgent and important, important but not urgent, urgent but not important, and neither. Focus on important tasks first.
- **MITs (Most Important Tasks):** Identify 2-3 key tasks you must complete daily. Focus on these first before moving on to less critical tasks.

5. Minimize Distractions

Staying focused is critical to managing your time effectively. Here's how to minimize distractions:

- **Dedicated Workspace:** Set up a specific area for work that's free from distractions.
- **Turn Off Notifications:** Silence non-essential notifications on your phone and computer during work hours.
- **Set Boundaries:** Let your family or roommates know about your work schedule and ask them to keep interruptions to a minimum during those hours. This way, you can stay focused and get the most out of your work time.

How to Remain Productive as a Remote Worker

Working remotely offers incredible flexibility and freedom, but it also comes with unique challenges when staying productive. Without a traditional office structure, it's easy to get distracted or lose focus.

1. Establish a Routine

A daily routine is essential for staying productive as a remote worker. It gives your day a structured flow, helping you start work on time and stick to a consistent schedule.

A routine keeps you in the groove, making it easier to switch between tasks and manage your time effectively.

Plus, having a set routine can help create a sense of normalcy and balance so you're more focused and motivated throughout the day. It's like giving your day a roadmap, guiding you toward a productive and fulfilling work experience.

Here are some steps to establish a productive routine:

- **Start Your Day Right:** Wake up at the same time every day, have a nutritious breakfast, and get dressed as if you're going to the office. This helps set a professional tone for your day.
- **Designate Work Hours:** Stick to a schedule that mirrors a traditional workday. This helps you stay disciplined and ensures you have clear boundaries between work and personal time.

2. Create a Dedicated Workspace

We've detailed the process of setting up your workspace in Chapter 3, but it's worth reiterating that a dedicated workspace is essential for maintaining productivity as a remote worker. It helps you establish a clear boundary between your work and personal life, fostering a professional mindset and minimizing distractions.

Having a specific spot solely for work can significantly boost your efficiency, keeping you organized and focused.

3. Stay Organized

Talking about workspaces, an organized workspace and workflow can save you time and reduce stress.

How to do it:

- **Declutter:** Keep your workspace tidy and free of unnecessary items.
- **Organize Files:** Use a consistent system for organizing digital files and emails. This makes it easier to find what you need quickly.
- **Task Lists:** Keep a running list of tasks and update it regularly. This helps you stay on top of what needs to be done.

4. Plan Your Day

Planning your day is critical to staying productive as a remote worker. It helps you map out what needs to be done and prioritize your tasks so you're not just reacting to whatever comes up.

Setting aside time for each task keeps you organized and focused, making it easier to tackle your to-do list efficiently.

A well-planned day can reduce stress and help you avoid last-minute rushes. With a clear plan, you can stay on top of your work and ensure you're using your time in the best way possible.

Tips to help you plan your day:

- **Make a To-Do List:** Start your day by listing out tasks. Prioritize them based on importance and urgency. Tackling the most critical tasks first can give you a sense of accomplishment early in the day.
- **Time Blocking:** Allocate specific time slots for different tasks. For example, dedicate 9:00 AM to 11:00 AM to focused work, then take a break, followed by meetings or administrative tasks in the afternoon.

5. Take Regular Breaks

Taking breaks is essential for staying productive as a remote worker. It may seem counterintuitive, but stepping away from your desk can boost your efficiency and creativity. Breaks allow your mind to recharge, helping you stay focused and avoid burnout.

6. Communicate Effectively

Clear communication helps you manage your time and collaborate efficiently with your team. We go into detail on how to collaborate effectively as a remote worker in the next chapter, but in the meantime, here are some tips:

- **Regular Check-Ins:** Schedule regular meetings with your team to discuss progress and align priorities.
- **Be Clear and Concise:** When communicating via email or messaging apps, be clear and to the point to avoid misunderstandings and reduce back-and-forth.
- **Use Collaboration Tools:** Tools like Slack, Microsoft Teams, or Zoom can help facilitate real-time communication and collaboration.

7. Reflect and Adapt

Regular reflection helps you understand what works best for you. Some methods you can apply are:

- **Assess Your Productivity:** At the end of each week, reflect on what went well and what didn't. Adjust your strategies accordingly.
- **Be Flexible:** Be bold and tweak your routine or try new productivity techniques. What works for one person might not work for another, so find what suits you best.

By implementing these time management strategies, you can maximize your productivity and enjoy the benefits of remote work without feeling overwhelmed. Remember, the key is to find a balance that works for you and allows you to stay focused, motivated, and productive.

Chapter 8:
Communication and Collaboration Tools & Strategies

Effective communication and collaboration are vital to thriving in a remote work environment. Unlike traditional office settings, remote work requires more effort to ensure everyone stays connected and productive.

In this chapter, we'll explore strategies for effective virtual communication, tools for team collaboration, and tips for managing time zone differences to keep your remote team running smoothly.

Effective Virtual Communication Strategies

Be Clear and Concise

Clear and concise communication is a powerful tool that reduces misunderstandings and ensures that everyone is on the same page. Mastering this skill will boost your confidence in your communication abilities.

How to Do It:

- **Use Simple Language**: Avoid jargon such as 'synergy' or 'leverage' and keep your messages straightforward.

- **Get to the Point**: Start with the main point and provide details as needed. This helps the recipient quickly understand the key message.

Choose the Right Communication Channel

Different types of communication are suited to specific channels.

How to Choose:

- **Email**: Best for detailed or formal communication requiring a record or reference.

- **Instant Messaging**: This is ideal for quick, informal chats or updates. Tools like Slack or Microsoft Teams are great for real-time conversations.

- **Video Calls:** are Useful for meetings, brainstorming sessions, or discussions that benefit from face-to-face interaction. Platforms like Zoom or Google Meet are popular choices.

Set Communication Guidelines

Guidelines play a crucial role in managing expectations and ensuring smooth communication. They provide a structured framework that reassures everyone about the workflow.

How to Set Guidelines:

- **Response Times**: Agree on expected response times for different types of communication (e.g., within 24 hours for emails).
- **Availability**: Share your working hours and preferred methods for urgent matters so your team knows how to reach you when needed.

Tools for Team Collaboration

Project Management Tools

These tools help track progress, assign tasks, and keep everyone organized.

Popular Options:

- **Trello**: Uses boards and cards to manage tasks and projects visually.
- **Asana**: Provides a more detailed task management system with features for deadlines, priorities, and task assignments.

Document Sharing and Collaboration

Collaborative tools make working together on documents, spreadsheets, and presentations easy.

Popular Options:

- **Google Workspace:** Includes Docs, Sheets, and Slides, which allow multiple users to edit and comment in real time.
- **Microsoft Office 365:** Offers features similar to Word, Excel, and PowerPoint, plus cloud storage with OneDrive.

Communication Platforms

These platforms facilitate daily interactions and help keep the team connected.

Popular Options:

- **Slack:** Offers channels for different topics, direct messaging, and integrations with other tools.

- **Microsoft Teams:** This comprehensive collaboration tool provides chat, video calls, and integration with Office apps.

Managing Time Zone Differences

Establish Overlapping Hours

Having overlapping working hours helps ensure that team members can communicate in real time.

How to Do It:

- **Find Common Ground:** Determine times when most team members are available and schedule meetings or collaborative sessions during these periods.

- **Be Flexible** with your schedule to accommodate different time zones when necessary is a key aspect of managing time zone differences. It makes you more adaptable and open-minded in your approach.

Use Scheduling Tools

Scheduling tools help manage and coordinate meetings across different time zones.

Popular Options:

- **World Time Buddy:** This allows you to compare time zones and find suitable meeting times.
- **Time Zone Converter:** A simple tool for converting time zones to ensure meetings are scheduled accurately.

Document and Share Key Information

Documentation ensures that everyone can access important information, even if they weren't present for a meeting.

How to Document:

- **Meeting Notes:** Summarize key points and decisions made during meetings and share them with the team.
- **Asynchronous Updates:** Use project management tools or shared documents to update everyone on progress and changes.

Implementing effective communication strategies, utilizing the right collaboration tools, and thoughtfully managing time zone differences can ensure smooth and productive interactions with your remote team.

These practices will help you stay connected and collaborate effectively, no matter where you or your team members are located.

Chapter 9:
Maintaining Work-Life Balance

Maintaining a healthy work-life balance can be challenging when working remotely, as the boundaries between work and personal life often blur. In this chapter, we'll explore practical strategies for setting boundaries, managing stress, and creating a daily routine that helps you stay balanced and productive.

Setting Boundaries Between Work and Personal Life

Create a Dedicated Workspace

Having a specific area for work helps you mentally separate work from personal life.

How to Do It:

- **Designate a Work Area:** Choose a room or a corner of your home where you work exclusively. Alternatively, you can rent a desk in a co-working facility. Ideally, this space should be distinct from your relaxation areas.
- **Use Work-Only Tools:** To reinforce the separation, keep work-related materials, like your computer and office supplies, in this area.

Establish Clear Work Hours

Setting specific work hours helps you maintain a routine and signal to others when you're available.

How to Do It:

- **Define Your Schedule**: Set consistent start and end times for your workday. Communicate these hours to your colleagues and family.
- **Stick to Your Hours**: Avoid checking work emails or taking calls outside your work hours. Use alarms or reminders to signal the end of your workday.

Communicate Boundaries

Letting others know your work boundaries helps minimize interruptions and sets clear expectations.

How to Do It:

- **Inform Your Family:** Explain your work schedule and the importance of minimizing distractions during work hours.

- **Set Expectations with Colleagues:** Let your team know your working hours and preferred communication times. When you're not available, use status updates or out-of-office messages.

Managing Stress and Preventing Burnout

Take Regular Breaks

Regular breaks help you recharge and maintain focus throughout the day.

How to Do It:

- **Use the Pomodoro Technique:** Work for 25 minutes, then take a 5-minute break. After doing this four times, enjoy a longer break of 15-30 minutes.

- **Step Away from Your Desk:** Use break times to stretch, take a walk, or do something you enjoy to refresh your mind and body.

Practice Stress-Relief Techniques

Managing stress helps prevent Burnout and improves overall well-being.

Techniques to Try:

- **Deep Breathing:** Take deep breaths to calm your mind and reduce stress.
- **Exercise:** Incorporate physical activity into your day, even if it's just a short walk or a few minutes of stretching.

- **Mindfulness and Meditation**: To manage stress and maintain focus, spend a few minutes practicing mindfulness or meditation each day.

Seek Support When Needed

Talking to others can provide perspective and support when you're feeling overwhelmed.

How to Seek Support:

- **Talk to Your Manager:** If work demands are causing stress, discuss possible adjustments or support with your manager.
- **Connect with Peers:** Share experiences with colleagues who may be facing similar challenges.

- **Consider Professional Help**: If stress becomes unmanageable, seek advice from a mental health professional or counsellor.

Creating a Healthy Daily Routine

Start Your Day with a Routine

A regular morning routine sets a positive tone for your day and helps you ease into work mode.

How to Create It:

- **Morning Rituals**: Incorporate activities like exercise, a healthy breakfast, or reading to start your day positively.
- **Set a Start Time**: Begin your workday at the same time each day to establish a routine.

Include Regular Physical Activity

Exercise boosts energy, improves mood, and helps you stay healthy.

How to Include It:

- **Schedule Workouts**: Set aside specific times for exercise, whether a morning jog, a lunchtime yoga session, or an evening workout.
- **Stay Active During the Day:** Take short movement breaks, such as stretching or walking, to keep your body active.

End Your Day with a Routine

A consistent end-of-day routine helps you transition from work to personal time and promotes relaxation.

How to Create It:

- **Wrap-Up Work**: Review your accomplishments and plan for the next day before finishing work.
- **Unwind**: To signal the end of your workday, engage in relaxing activities such as reading, cooking, or spending time with family.

Maintaining work-life balance while working remotely requires intentional effort and self-awareness. By setting clear boundaries, managing stress effectively, and creating a balanced daily routine, you can ensure that both your work and personal life remain fulfilling and productive.

PART IV: Advanced Remote Work Skills

Chapter 10:

Developing Technical Proficiency

In the world of remote work, having solid technical skills is crucial for staying productive and connected. Whether you're using sophisticated project management tools or troubleshooting a tech hiccup, being tech-savvy can make a big difference in your remote work experience.

In this chapter, we'll cover essential software and tools for remote work, troubleshooting common tech issues, and the importance of continuous learning and skill development.

Continuous Learning and Skill Development

Enhance Your Technical Skills

For remote workers, keeping your technical skills sharp is essential because it helps you stay competitive and adapt to new tools and technologies. As the tech landscape evolves, up-to-date skills ensure you can handle new challenges and make the most of the latest innovations.

Plus, continuously improving your abilities can open up new opportunities for career growth and make you a more valuable asset to your team.

How to Do It:

- **Take Online Courses:** Platforms like Coursera, Udemy, or LinkedIn Learning offer courses on various technical skills.
- **Practice Regularly:** Apply new skills in your work to reinforce learning and gain hands-on experience.

Seek Feedback and Improvement

For remote workers, seeking feedback and focusing on improvement is crucial because it helps you grow professionally and stay aligned with your team's goals. Regular feedback allows you to identify areas for growth, enhance your skills, and ensure you're meeting expectations.

Embracing constructive criticism and making improvements boosts your performance and shows your commitment to doing your best work, making you a more valuable team member.

How to Do It:

- **Request Feedback**: Ask colleagues or managers for feedback on your technical skills and improvement areas.
- **Set Learning Goals**: Create goals for learning or improving new skills, and track your progress.

Keeping Up with Industry Trends

In the fast-paced world of remote work, staying updated with the latest trends is not just beneficial—it's essential. Keeping up with industry trends helps you remain competitive, adapt to new technologies, and continuously improve your productivity.

Why It's Important to Keep Up with Trends

Stay Competitive

The remote work landscape constantly evolves with new tools, practices, and technologies.

How It Helps

> By staying updated, you ensure you use the most effective tools and methods, which helps you stay relevant and competitive in your field. This can make you more attractive to employers or clients looking for cutting-edge skills and knowledge.

Enhance productivity

New technologies and tools often involve improvements designed to enhance productivity and streamline workflows.

How It Helps

> Adopting the latest tools and techniques can help you work more efficiently, save time, and achieve better results. This can be particularly important in a remote setting where you rely on digital solutions to manage your work.

Adapt to Changes

Remote work trends and technologies can change rapidly, from new communication tools to evolving best practices.

How It Helps

> Keeping up with these changes allows you to adapt quickly, minimizing disruptions to your workflow and ensuring that you're always prepared for shifts in the remote work environment.

Professional Growth

Continuous learning and adaptation are crucial for career development and personal growth.

How It Helps

> Engaging with current trends provides opportunities for skill enhancement and knowledge expansion, contributing to your professional growth and increasing your value in the job market.

How to Keep Up with Trends

1. Follow Industry News and Blogs

Industry news and blogs often cover the latest developments, emerging technologies, and best practices.

How to Do It:

- **Subscribe to Newsletters**: Sign up for newsletters from industry leaders, remote work experts, and technology providers.
- **Read Reputable Blogs**: Follow blogs from well-known platforms such as Harvard Business Review, TechCrunch, or Remote.co.

2. Join Online Communities and Forums

Online communities and forums are valuable sources of real-time information and peer insights.

How to Do It:

- **Participate in Forums**: Engage in discussions on platforms like Reddit, Quora, or specialized forums related to your field.
- **Join Professional Groups**: Connect with professional groups on LinkedIn or Facebook to share knowledge and stay informed about industry changes.

3. Attend Webinars and Virtual Conferences

Webinars and virtual conferences provide in-depth knowledge of new trends, tools, and practices from experts in the field.

How to Do It:

- **Register for Events**: Look for webinars, workshops, or virtual conferences related to remote work or your industry.
- **Watch Recorded Sessions**: If you can't attend live, many events offer recorded sessions you can watch at your convenience.

4. Take Online Courses and Certifications

Online courses and certifications offer structured learning on new tools, technologies, and methodologies.

How to Do It:

- **Enroll in Courses**: Platforms like Coursera, Udemy, or LinkedIn Learning offer courses on various topics.
- **Earn Certifications**: Consider earning certifications demonstrating your proficiency in new tools or technologies relevant to remote work.

5. Network with Peers and Mentors

Connecting with peers and mentors lets you learn from their experiences and get valuable insights into industry trends.

How to Do It:

- **Attend Networking Events**: Participate in virtual meetups or networking events to connect with others in your field.
- **Seek Mentorship**: Find a mentor who can provide guidance on career development and industry trends.

6. Experiment with New Tools

Hands-on experience with new tools and technologies helps you understand their potential benefits and applications.

How to Do It:

- **Try Free Versions:** Many tools offer free versions or trials, allowing you to explore their features without committing financially.
- **Evaluate and Integrate:** Test out new tools in your workflow and assess their impact on your productivity and efficiency.

Staying current with trends in remote work helps you remain agile and proactive in an ever-changing environment.

By following industry news, participating in professional communities, and continuously learning, you can enhance your skills, adapt to new developments, and ensure that you're making the most of your remote work experience.

Chapter 11:
Building a Remote Work Community

One of the unique challenges of remote work is staying connected and feeling part of a community. Unlike traditional office environments, which offer spontaneous interactions and face-to-face networking opportunities, remote work requires a more proactive approach to building relationships and finding support.

In this chapter, we'll explore how to network with other remote workers, participate in virtual events and conferences, and find mentorship and support to create a vibrant remote work community.

Networking with Other Remote Workers

Leverage Online Communities

Online communities provide opportunities to connect with other remote professionals, share experiences, and gain insights.

How to Do It:

- **Join Relevant Forums:** Participate in forums like Reddit's r/remote, or specialized groups on Facebook and LinkedIn. These platforms often have dedicated spaces for remote workers to discuss challenges and opportunities.

- **Engage in Discussions**: Don't just lurk—jump in and join the discussions! Ask questions and share your own advice and experiences. To maintain these relationships, consider following up on previous discussions, sharing relevant resources, or even arranging virtual coffee chats with your connections.

Attend Meetups and Virtual Group Meetings

Meetups offer a chance to connect with others in similar fields or with similar interests.

How to Do It:

- **Join Professional Networks:** Engage with professional organizations or networks related to your field, as they often offer virtual networking opportunities.

- **Search for Meetups:** Look for virtual meetups on platforms like Meetup.com or Eventbrite. When attending these meetups, be proactive in introducing yourself, asking questions, and exchanging contact information with other participants to make the most of your networking opportunities.

Build Relationships on Social Media

Social media can be a great way to build and keep professional relationships.

How to Do It:

- **Follow Influencers and Thought Leaders:** Connect with industry leaders on X, LinkedIn, or other platforms to stay informed and engage in discussions.

- **Participate in Relevant Hashtags**: Use and follow hashtags related to remote work, freelancing, or your industry to discover and join conversations.

Participating in Virtual Events and Conferences

Virtual events and conferences not only provide valuable learning opportunities and professional growth, but also a sense of belonging and inclusion in a larger community of remote professionals.

How to Do It:

- **Search for Industry-Specific Conferences:** Look for online conferences and events relevant to your field. Websites like Eventbrite or industry-specific sites often list upcoming virtual events.

- **Attend Workshops and Webinars:** Participate in workshops or webinars to gain new skills and insights relevant to your remote work.

Engage with Speakers and Attendees

Engaging with others during events helps you make meaningful connections and gain valuable insights.

How to Do It:

- **Ask Questions:** During Q&A sessions, ask questions to speakers and engage in discussions to gain deeper insights. After the event, consider reaching out to the speakers or other attendees via email or social media to continue the conversation and build a lasting connection.

- **Network with Attendees**: Use chat features or networking sessions to connect with other attendees. Follow up with them after the event to continue the conversation.

Leverage Event Platforms

Event platforms often have features that facilitate networking and interaction.

How to Do It:

- **Explore Event Apps**: Many virtual events use apps or platforms that offer networking features, such as virtual "coffee chats" or message boards. Use these tools to connect with other participants.
- **Download Resources**: To extend your learning beyond the event, use any available materials, such as presentation slides or recorded sessions.

Finding Mentorship and Support

Mentors, with their guidance, support, and advice, empower you to navigate challenges and grow professionally, instilling a sense of confidence and capability.

How to Do It:

- **Identify Potential Mentors:** Look for experienced professionals with a track record of success in your field. You can find them through LinkedIn, professional organizations, or recommendations from your network.

- **Reach Out:** Politely reach out to potential mentors with a clear request for mentorship. Explain why you admire their work and how you believe they could help you. Remember, everyone is busy, so start with a small request, like a 15-minute meeting or asking a specific question they can answer at their convenience.

Join Professional Support Groups

Support groups, by offering a space to share experiences, seek advice, and find encouragement, provide a sense of comfort and reassurance, making you feel secure and supported in your remote work journey.

How to Do It:

- **Look for Support Groups:** Search for support groups related to remote work or your specific industry. These can often be found on social media platforms, forums, or through professional organizations.

- **Participate Actively:** Engage actively in discussions and offer support to others. Building relationships in these groups can provide mutual support and valuable connections.

Utilize Online Resources

Online resources can offer advice, community support, and opportunities for professional development.

How to Do It:

- **Explore Online Courses and Forums:** Take advantage of online courses and forums offering remote workers support and guidance.
- **Follow Relevant Blogs and Podcasts:** Subscribe to blogs and podcasts that provide remote work and professional development insights and advice.

Building a solid remote work community requires effort and intentionality, but it's incredibly rewarding.

By networking with other remote workers, participating in virtual events, and finding mentorship and support, you'll create a network that enriches your remote work experience and helps you thrive in a flexible work environment.

Chapter 12:

Remote Work Etiquette and Professionalism

Remote work brings flexibility and freedom but also requires a strong sense of Professionalism and good etiquette to ensure smooth interactions and effective collaboration. In this chapter, we'll cover best practices for virtual meetings, effective communication with remote teams, and maintaining Professionalism in a remote environment.

Prepare Ahead of Time

Preparation is the key to ensuring that meetings run smoothly and stay focused. It sets the tone for the meeting and ensures its efficiency.

How to Do It:

- **Set an Agenda**: Before the meeting, share a clear agenda with all participants. This helps everyone understand the topics to be discussed and come prepared.
- **Test Your Tech**: To avoid technical issues during the meeting, check your internet connection, camera, and microphone.

Be Punctual and Respectful

Timeliness and respect show Professionalism and help keep meetings efficient.

How to Do It:

- **Join on Time:** Log in to the meeting a few minutes early to address any last-minute issues.

- **Mute When Not Speaking**: Mute your microphone when you're not speaking to reduce background noise and interruptions.

Engage and Participate Actively

Active participation is not just about speaking up; it's about ensuring all viewpoints are considered and making meetings more productive and inclusive.

How to Do It:

- **Use Video When Possible:** Enable your camera to maintain a more personal and engaging connection with other participants.
- **Contribute to Discussions:** Share your thoughts and feedback, and be attentive to others' contributions. Use chat functions to ask questions or make comments without interrupting.

Follow Up with Clear Actions

Summarizing and following up on action items is crucial. It ensures that tasks are completed and decisions are implemented, maintaining the meeting's momentum.

How to Do It:

- **Send Meeting Notes:** After the meeting, summarize key points and action items to all participants.
- **Set Deadlines:** Clearly outline who is responsible for what tasks and set deadlines to ensure accountability.

Communicating Effectively with Remote Teams

Be Clear and Concise

Clear communication is the key to minimizing misunderstandings and keeping everyone aligned, providing a sense of reassurance and confidence in your remote work.

How to Do It:

- **Use Simple Language:** Avoid jargon and overly complex language in your messages.

- **Get to the Point:** State the main message or request upfront and provide additional details as needed.

Choose the Right Communication Channel

Different types of communication are best suited to different channels.

How to Do It:

- **Use Email for Formal Communication:** Email is a good choice for detailed or formal messages.
- **Use Instant Messaging for Quick Updates:** Tools like Slack or Microsoft Teams are great for informal, real-time communication.

Be Responsive and Reliable

Timely responses and reliability build trust and keep projects moving forward.

How to Do It:

- **Set Expectations for Response Times:** Tell your team when to expect a response, and stick to these timelines.
- **Follow Through on Promises:** If you commit to a task or deadline, ensure you complete it as promised.

Show Appreciation and Positivity

Positive communication fosters a supportive and collaborative team environment.

How to Do It:

- **Acknowledge Contributions:** Recognize and thank team members for their work and efforts.
- **Maintain a Positive Tone:** Use encouraging and constructive language, especially when providing feedback.

Maintaining Professionalism in a Remote Environment

Dress Appropriately

Even if you're working from home, dressing up helps maintain a professional mindset and appearance.

How to Do It:

- **Follow Dress Codes**: Adhere to any dress codes set by your organization for video calls or virtual meetings.
- **Dress for Success**: If you participate in a video meeting or represent your company, wear business-casual attire (at least on top).

Create a Professional Workspace

A dedicated workspace helps you stay organized and focused and maintains a professional appearance during video calls.

How to Do It:

- **Designate a Work Area:** Set up a specific area for work that is free from distractions and clutter.

- **Ensure a Professional Background:** If you're using video calls, ensure your background is clean and professional. Use virtual backgrounds if necessary.

Maintain Work-Life Balance

Keeping a clear boundary between work and personal life helps maintain Professionalism and prevents Burnout.

How to Do It:

- **Set Work Hours:** Define and stick to regular working hours to separate work from personal time.
- **Avoid Overworking:** Respect your own time and avoid working beyond your scheduled hours.

Respect Confidentiality and Privacy

Protecting sensitive information and respecting privacy maintains trust and Professionalism.

How to Do It:

- **Secure Your Devices:** Use strong passwords and security measures to protect work-related information.

- **Be Mindful of Confidentiality**: Avoid discussing sensitive information in public spaces or with unauthorized individuals.
- **Consider using a VPN:** When working remotely, it is a smart move because it helps keep your internet connection secure and private.

A VPN, or Virtual Private Network, encrypts your data, making it much harder for hackers to access sensitive information. It also allows you to access company resources safely, even on public Wi-Fi. Overall, a VPN adds extra protection and peace of mind while you work from anywhere. Some companies offer VPN; you can ask your IT team if they provide this setup.

Maintaining etiquette and Professionalism in a remote work environment is essential for effective collaboration and personal success. By following these best practices for virtual meetings, communicating clearly, and upholding Professionalism, you'll contribute to a positive and productive remote work experience.

PART V: Long-Term Success and Growth

Chapter 13:
Career Development in a Remote World

Remote work offers flexibility and a unique work environment. Still, it also comes with its own set of challenges regarding career development. How do you set goals, seek promotions, and build a personal brand while working from home? This chapter will guide you through setting career goals, seeking new opportunities, and creating a personal brand in the remote world.

Setting Career Goals and Planning Your Path

Define Your Career Aspirations

Having clear career goals helps you focus your efforts and make intelligent decisions about your career journey.

How to Do It:

- **Reflect on Your Interests**: Think about what excites you in your field and what you want to achieve. This could be a particular role, skill, or project you're passionate about.

- **Set Specific Goals**: Create SMART goals (Specific, Measurable, Achievable, Relevant, Time-bound). For example, "I want to improve my project management skills by completing a certification course within the next six months."

Create a Career Development Plan

A structured plan helps you stay on track and measure your progress toward your career goals.

How to Do It:

- **Identify Key Milestones:** Break your goals into smaller, manageable milestones. For example, suppose your goal is to become a team leader. In that case, milestones include gaining relevant experience, taking leadership training, and seeking feedback from peers.

- **Set Timelines:** Determine when you aim to achieve each milestone. This will help keep you motivated and stay focused on your goals.

Regularly Review and Adjust Your Plan

Your career goals and circumstances might change, so staying flexible is essential.

How to Do It:

- **Schedule Check-Ins:** Set aside time every few months to review your progress and adjust your goals or plan as needed.

- **Seek Feedback:** Ask for feedback from mentors or supervisors to get an external perspective on your progress and areas for improvement.

Seeking Promotions and New Opportunities

Demonstrate Your Value

Showing your value helps position you as a candidate for promotions and new opportunities.

How to Do It:

- **Track Your Achievements**: Record your accomplishments, such as successful projects, innovations, or improvements. This can be useful during performance reviews or promotion discussions.

- **Communicate Results**: Share your achievements with your team and supervisors regularly. Use data and specific examples to highlight the impact of your work.

Express Your Career Ambitions

Letting your supervisors and colleagues know about your career goals can open new opportunities.

How to Do It:

- **Have Regular Conversations:** Discuss your career aspirations with your manager during performance reviews or one-on-one meetings. Let them know you're interested in taking on more responsibility or exploring new roles.

- **Seek Opportunities for Growth:** Volunteer for new projects or cross-functional teams that align with your career goals. This shows initiative and helps you build skills relevant to your desired role.

Build Skills and Gain Experience

Acquiring new skills and experience makes you a stronger candidate for promotions and new roles.

How to Do It:

- **Take Advantage of Training**: Participate in training programs, workshops, or courses that enhance your skills and knowledge.
- **Pursue Stretch Assignments**: Seek out challenging projects or tasks that push you out of your comfort zone and help you gain experience in areas you want to grow.

Building a Personal Brand

Define Your Unique Value Proposition

A strong personal brand helps you stand out and communicates your unique skills and strengths.

How to Do It:

- **Identify Your Strengths**: Reflect on your skills, experiences, and achievements. Consider what sets you apart from others in your field.
- **Craft Your Elevator Pitch**: Create a concise and compelling summary of who you are, what you do, and what you're passionate about. This can be useful for networking and personal branding.

Enhance Your Online Presence

Having a strong online presence helps you build credibility and connect with others in your industry. When you share your work, ideas, and experiences online, people see you as an expert in your field.

It also makes it easier to network with peers, learn from others, and stay updated on industry trends. Whether it's through LinkedIn, a personal blog, or social media, being active online can open up new opportunities and help you grow professionally.

How to Do It:

- **Optimize Your LinkedIn Profile:** Ensure your LinkedIn profile is up-to-date with a professional photo, detailed work experience, and endorsements for your skills.

- **Share Your Expertise**: Write articles, share insights, or post updates related to your field on LinkedIn or other relevant platforms. This showcases your knowledge and positions you as a thought leader.

Network and Build Relationships

Building a network helps you establish connections and opens up opportunities for collaboration and advancement.

How to Do It:

- **Attend Industry Event:** Connect with other professionals in your field by participating in virtual conferences, webinars, or online networking events.

- **Engage with Influencers**: Follow and interact with industry leaders and influencers. Comment on their posts and share relevant content to increase your visibility.

Stay Consistent and Authentic

Consistency and authenticity in your personal brand help build trust and credibility.

How to Do It:

- **Be Genuine:** Ensure that your personal brand accurately reflects who you are and what you stand for. Authenticity helps build stronger connections with others.

- **Maintain Consistency:** Keep your messaging, tone, and online presence consistent across all platforms to reinforce your personal brand.

By setting clear career goals, seeking out new opportunities, and building a strong personal brand, you'll be well-positioned for growth and success in the remote work world.

Embrace these strategies to navigate your career development effectively and make the most of the unique opportunities that remote work offers.

Chapter 14:
Managing Your Finances as a Remote Worker

Managing finances can be one of the most challenging aspects of remote work and digital nomadism. Whether working from home or exploring new destinations, having a solid financial plan is crucial for stability and peace of mind. This chapter will cover essential financial tips for remote workers and digital nomads, including budgeting, income management, and tax planning.

Quick disclaimer: the following content is meant to be used as a guide only. For your specific financial needs, make sure to consult a certified Financial Advisor.

Budgeting for Remote Work

Budgeting allows you to track and control your expenses, preventing overspending and helping you save for important goals.

Budgeting is crucial for remote workers because it helps manage the ups and downs of irregular income income. It ensures you can cover your expenses even during slower periods. It saves you money for taxes, emergencies, and professional development.

Budgeting provides financial stability and peace of mind by keeping track of your spending and saving for your goals, making your remote work journey smoother and more enjoyable.

Track Your Income and Expenses

Knowing where your money is coming from and going helps you manage your finances more effectively.

How to Do It:

- **Use Budgeting Apps**: Tools like Mint or YNAB (You Need A Budget) can help you track your income, expenses, and savings goals.

- **Create a Simple Spreadsheet**: A basic spreadsheet can help you categorize and monitor your spending if you prefer a more hands-on approach.

Plan for Fluctuating Income

Remote work, mainly freelance or contract work, can result in irregular income. Unlike traditional jobs with steady paychecks, freelance income can fluctuate. Budgeting helps you manage these ups and downs, ensuring you can cover expenses even during lean periods.

How to Do It:

- **Build an Emergency Fund:** Save at least three to six months' worth of expenses to cover periods of low-income income or unexpected costs.
- **Set Up a Budget Buffer:** Allocate a portion of your monthly income to a buffer account to smooth out fluctuations.

Consider the Local Cost of Living

As a remote worker, it's essential to consider the local cost of living because it affects how far your income will go. Living in a city with a high cost of living can mean higher rent, groceries, and other expenses, which might quickly eat into your budget.

On the other hand, choosing a place with a lower cost of living can help your money stretch further, allowing you to save more or enjoy a better lifestyle. By being mindful of these differences, you can make smarter financial decisions and find a location that suits your budget and needs.

How to Do It:

- **Research Costs**: Use tools like Numbeo or Expatistan to compare living costs in different cities or countries.
- **Adjust Your Budget**: Modify your budget based on the local cost of living to ensure you stay within your means.

Managing Income

Set Up Multiple Income Streams

Setting up multiple income streams as a remote worker is smart because it adds financial security and stability. Relying on just one source of Income can be risky, significantly if work slows down or a project ends unexpectedly.

Various income streams—like freelance gigs, passive income income, or part-time jobs—ensure you have money coming in from different places. This helps cover your expenses and provides a cushion during lean times, giving you more peace of mind and financial freedom.

How to Do It:

- **Diversify Your Work**: Consider taking on different projects or clients to spread your income sources.
- **Explore Passive Income**: Explore opportunities to build additional income streams by creating digital products, affiliate marketing, or investing.

Invoice and Payment Management

Efficiently managing invoices and payments ensures timely income and financial stability.

Remote workers must know that effective invoice and payment management is critical to ensuring they get paid on time and keeping their finances in order. Creating clear, professional invoices that outline the work done, payment terms, and due dates is essential. Tools like invoicing software can help automate this process and send reminders for overdue payments.

Additionally, keeping track of all payments received and outstanding invoices helps you stay organized and avoid cash flow issues. By managing your invoices and payments well, you can focus more on your work and less on chasing payments.

How to Do It:

- **Use Invoicing Tools**: FreshBooks or QuickBooks can help you create professional invoices and track payments.
- **Follow Up on Payments**: Set reminders to follow up on overdue invoices and maintain a clear record of all transactions.

Consider Currency Exchange

Understanding currency exchanges and fees is crucial for remote workers who earn money in different currencies or work with clients worldwide.

Currency exchange rates can fluctuate, affecting how much you receive when converting your earnings into your local currency.

Additionally, banks and payment platforms often charge fees for currency conversions, which can add up over time.

By keeping an eye on exchange rates and choosing payment methods with low fees, you can maximize your income and manage your finances more effectively. This way, you can avoid surprises and ensure you get the most value from your earnings.

How to Do It:

- **Use Currency Conversion Tools**: Apps like XE Currency Converter can help you keep track of exchange rates.
- **Open Multi-Currency Accounts**: Some banks and online services offer multi-currency accounts to reduce conversion fees.

Planning for Taxes

Understand Tax Obligations

For remote workers, planning for taxes, especially in different countries, is important because it helps avoid surprises and ensures you meet all your tax obligations. Depending on where you live and where your clients are based, you might need to pay taxes in multiple places or deal with different tax rules.

By understanding the tax requirements of both your home country and any other countries where you do business, you can plan ahead, set aside the right amount of money, and avoid penalties. This proactive approach makes managing your finances smoother and keeps you on the right side of the law.

How to Do It:

- **Research Tax Laws:** Familiarize yourself with the tax regulations in your home country and any other country where you work.

- **Consult a Tax Professional:** To ensure you meet all obligations, consider working with a tax advisor specializing in international tax issues.

Keep Accurate Records

For remote workers, keeping accurate records is essential for smooth tax preparation and to avoid any last-minute stress. By tracking all your income, expenses, and receipts throughout the year, you'll have everything you need when tax season comes around. This organized approach helps you claim eligible deductions and ensures you're reporting your earnings correctly.

Accurate records also make handling audits or queries from tax authorities easier. In short, staying organized with your records simplifies tax time and helps you stay on top of your financial game.

How to Do It:

- **Document All Expenses**: Keep receipts and records of all business-related expenses for tax deduction purposes.

- **Organize Financial Documents**: Organize your tax documents and financial records using digital tools or a dedicated filing system.

Plan for Quarterly Payments

Many countries require freelancers and self-employed individuals to make estimated quarterly tax payments. For remote workers, planning for quarterly tax payments is essential because it helps you stay on top of your tax obligations and avoid a big tax bill at the end of the year.

Since freelancers and remote workers often don't have taxes automatically deducted from their income, tax authorities might expect you to make estimated payments four times a year.

By setting aside money regularly and paying these quarterly estimates, you can manage your cash flow better, reduce the risk of penalties, and keep your finances in good shape. It's a simple way to stay organized and prevent surprises when tax season arrives.

How to Do It:

- **Calculate Estimated Taxes:** Use tax calculators or consult a tax professional to estimate your quarterly payments.
- **Set Aside Funds:** Allocate a portion of your monthly income for tax payments to avoid surprises.

Managing finances as a remote worker or digital nomad requires careful planning and organization. By tracking income and expenses, managing irregular Income, understanding tax obligations, and staying on top of currency exchanges, you can ensure financial stability and focus on enjoying the flexibility and adventure of remote work.

Chapter 15:
Embracing a Remote Work Lifestyle

One of the greatest perks of remote work is the empowerment it offers to shape your work environment and lifestyle according to your preferences. Whether you travel while you work, balance work with personal passions, or draw inspiration from others who've successfully navigated this path, embracing a remote work lifestyle can be incredibly rewarding.

In this chapter, we'll explore how to make the most of this flexibility, including travelling while working and finding balance with your personal passions.

Travelling and Working from Anywhere

Combine Assignment with Adventure

Travelling while working can add excitement to your routine and allow you to experience new cultures and environments.

Combining work assignments with adventure while travelling as a remote worker is essential for a fulfilling experience. It allows you to stay productive and meet your work commitments while enjoying the excitement of new places and cultures.

How to Do It:

- **Choose Your Destinations Wisely:** Consider factors like internet connectivity, time zone differences, and local amenities (such as co-working spaces, cafes with good Wi-Fi, or libraries) when selecting places to work from. Destinations with reliable Wi-Fi and comfortable workspaces are ideal.

- **Plan Your Work Schedule:** Be mindful of time zone differences and ensure your work schedule aligns with your clients' or team's expectations. Use tools like world clocks (such as Time Buddy or World Time Buddy) and scheduling apps (such as Trello or Asana) to manage your time effectively.

Set Up a Mobile Office

A portable and functional workspace is crucial for maintaining productivity while travelling. Setting up a mobile office when travelling as a remote worker is essential for staying productive and organized.

A good mobile office means you have everything you need to work efficiently, no matter where you are. It helps you create a consistent work environment, making it easier to focus and finish tasks. Plus, with a reliable setup, you can avoid the stress of hunting for a suitable workspace each day, giving you more time to enjoy your travels.

How to Do It:

- **Invest in Portable Tech:** To stay connected, equip yourself with a lightweight laptop, noise-cancelling headphones, and a reliable mobile hotspot.
- **Create a Mobile Workspace:** Use travel-friendly accessories like a compact laptop stand, a foldable keyboard, and a portable mouse to set up a comfortable work environment wherever you are.

Travelling Ethically and Responsibly as a Digital Nomad

Travelling the world as a digital nomad is a fantastic chance to explore new places, experience different cultures, and meet people from all backgrounds.

However, with this freedom comes the responsibility to travel in a way that respects both the environment and the communities you visit.

Here's are some guidelines to help you travel ethically while in your remote work adventure:

1. Respect Local Cultures and Communities

Learn About Local Customs

Understanding and respecting local customs helps you blend in and show appreciation for the culture.

How to Do It:

- **Research Before You Go:** Spend some time learning about your visiting places' traditions, social norms, and etiquette. Guidebooks, local blogs, and travel forums are great resources.

- **Observe and Adapt:** Listen to how locals behave and follow their lead. Simple actions like dressing appropriately, being mindful of local dining customs, and learning a few phrases in the local language can make a big difference.

Support Local Businesses

Supporting local businesses helps boost the local economy and fosters positive relationships with the community.

How to Do It:

- **Eat Local:** Choose local restaurants, markets, and street vendors over international chains. This will support local entrepreneurs and allow you to experience authentic cuisine.

- **Shop Locally:** Buy souvenirs and necessities from local shops rather than large retailers. This helps keep money within the community and supports small business owners.

Be Mindful of Your Impact

Your actions can significantly impact the local environment and community.

How to Do It:

- **Avoid Disruptive Behaviour:** Be considerate of local practices and avoid activities that could be disruptive or disrespectful, such as loud noise or public displays of affection.

- **Minimize Waste:** Reduce your use of single-use plastics and dispose of waste properly. Participate in recycling programs where available.

2. Protect the Environment

Travel Sustainably

Sustainable travel practices help preserve natural resources and reduce your carbon footprint.

How to Do It:

- **Choose Eco-Friendly Transportation:** Instead of renting a car, opt for public transportation, biking, or walking. When flying, consider offsetting your carbon emissions through programs that support environmental projects. This means investing in projects that reduce greenhouse gas emissions, such as renewable energy or reforestation, to balance out the emissions from your flight.

- **Stay in Eco-Conscious Accommodations:** Look for accommodations with green certifications or implementing sustainable practices, such as reducing energy and water usage.

Respect Natural Spaces

Natural environments are fragile and deserve protection to preserve their beauty and biodiversity.

How to Do It:

- **Follow the "Leave No Trace" Principles:** Stay on marked trails, pack out all trash, and avoid picking plants or disturbing wildlife.//
- **Participate in Conservation Efforts:** If available, join local conservation activities or clean-up events. Even small efforts can contribute to the preservation of natural spaces.

Be Mindful of Wildlife

Interacting with wildlife can have unintended consequences for animals and their habitats.

How to Do It:

- **Observe from a Distance:** Enjoy wildlife without disturbing its natural behaviours or habitat. Avoid feeding animals or trying to interact with them.
- **Support Ethical Wildlife Tours:** Choose tours that prioritize animal welfare and conservation over exploitation.

3. Foster Positive Connections

Engage with the Local Community

Building relationships with local people enriches your travel experience and fosters mutual respect.

How to Do It:

- **Participate in Community Activities:** Join local events, classes, or workshops to learn more about the community and meet locals.

- **Volunteer:** Offer your skills or time to local organizations or causes. This can be a meaningful way to contribute to the community and gain deeper insights into local issues.

Practice Responsible Tourism

Responsible tourism helps ensure that your presence benefits the community rather than causing harm.

How to Do It:

- **Be a Respectful Guest:** Treat everyone with kindness and respect. Follow local guidelines and rules, especially when visiting sacred or sensitive sites.
- **Support Ethical Tourism Operators:** Choose tour operators and service providers demonstrating a commitment to ethical and sustainable practices.

Share Your Experiences Thoughtfully

Sharing your travel experiences responsibly helps raise awareness about ethical practices and encourages others to follow suit.

How to Do It:

- **Highlight Positive Practices:** When sharing travel stories or recommendations, emphasize the ethical and sustainable practices of the places and businesses you visited.
- **Use Your Platform for Good:** Use your blog, social media, or other platforms to advocate for responsible travel and raise awareness about important issues.

By embracing these ethical and responsible travel principles, you'll enhance your experience as a digital nomad and contribute positively to the places you visit.

Remember, travelling with respect and consideration helps preserve the beauty and culture of destinations for future travellers and locals alike.

Balance Work and Exploration

When travelling as a remote worker, balancing work and exploration is key. It lets you enjoy new places and experiences while staying caught up on your job.

Setting precise work hours allows you to remain productive and use your free time to explore, relax, and dive into the local culture. This way, you get the best of both worlds—keeping up with your work while making the most of your travel adventures.

Integrate Your Interests

Balancing work with personal passions helps maintain motivation and prevents burnout.

How to Do It:

- **Set Clear Boundaries:** Establish specific work hours and stick to them. Use tools like calendar reminders to keep track of your work commitments.

- **Schedule Downtime:** Plan time for exploring, relaxing, and enjoying local attractions. Make the most of your travels by immersing yourself in the local culture during your off-hours.

- **Allocate Time for Hobbies:** Set aside dedicated time each week for your hobbies and interests, whether painting, writing, or playing an instrument. This helps you stay balanced and fulfilled.

- **Find Synergies:** Look for ways to integrate your passions into your work. For example, if you love photography, consider incorporating it into your marketing or social media efforts.

Create a Flexible Routine

A flexible routine allows you to adjust your schedule to accommodate both work and personal interests.

How to Do It:

- **Design Your Ideal Workday:** Structure your workday to include blocks of time for both professional tasks and personal activities. For instance, you might work in the morning and take time in the afternoon for a workout or creative project.

- **Prioritize Self-Care**: Include self-care in your routine. This could include practices like meditation, exercise, or spending time with loved ones. A balanced routine supports overall well-being and productivity.

Set Goals for Personal Growth

Setting goals for personal passions ensures you continue to grow and develop outside of your professional life.

How to Do It:

- **Define Your Passion Projects:** Identify personal projects or goals you want to achieve, such as learning a new skill, completing a creative project, or participating in a local event.

- **Track Your Progress:** Regularly review your progress toward personal goals and celebrate your achievements. This helps keep you motivated and focused.

Embracing a remote work lifestyle means more than just working from home—leveraging the flexibility to live a fulfilling and balanced life.

By travelling while working, integrating your passions into your routine, and learning from successful remote workers, you can make the most of the unique opportunities that remote work offers.

Conclusion

As we wrap up this guide to thriving in remote work, let's reflect on the journey you've embarked on and look forward to the opportunities ahead.

Reflecting on Your Remote Work Journey

Starting out as a remote worker or digital nomad is an exciting adventure full of possibilities. From setting up your home office to mastering the art of virtual communication, you've learned how to adapt and excel in a remote work environment. You've navigated through budgeting, understood the importance of maintaining a work-life balance, and embraced the freedom of working from anywhere.

Think back to where you started and celebrate the progress you've made. You've tackled challenges, discovered new ways to stay productive, and perhaps even experienced the joy of travelling while working. This journey is unique to each individual, and every step you've taken has contributed to your growth and success.

Encouragement and Motivation for Continuous Improvement

Remote work is a dynamic field that continues to evolve. Embracing this lifestyle means continuously seeking ways to improve and adapt. Remember, growth often comes from stepping outside your comfort zone and trying new approaches. It is important to:

- **Stay Curious:** Keep learning about new tools, trends, and techniques that can enhance your remote work experience. Whether it's a new productivity app or a fresh approach to managing your time, staying curious will keep you ahead of the curve.

- **Seek Feedback:** Regularly ask colleagues, mentors, or clients for feedback. Constructive feedback can provide valuable insights and help you refine your skills and strategies.

- **Set New Goals:** As you achieve your current goals, set new ones to keep pushing yourself forward. Whether advancing in your career, improving your work environment, or exploring new places, ongoing goal-setting ensures you're constantly growing.

Embracing remote work is not just about adapting to a new way of working; it's about creating a fulfilling and balanced lifestyle that aligns with your personal and professional aspirations. By applying the strategies and tips outlined in this book, you've laid a strong foundation for a successful remote career.

As you continue your remote work journey, remember that flexibility, resilience, and a positive mindset are your greatest assets. Embrace each new challenge as an opportunity to learn and grow. With the right approach, remote work can offer a fulfilling career and a lifestyle that allows you to thrive both personally and professionally.

Thank you for joining me on this journey. Here's to your continued success and enjoyment in remote work.

www.ingramcontent.com/pod-product-compliance
Lightning Source LLC
Chambersburg PA
CBHW031618210526
45464CB00004B/1645